The
Red-Tailed Hawk

by Lola Schaefer
illustrated by Stephen Taylor

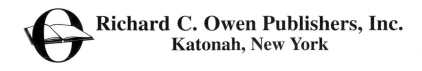

Richard C. Owen Publishers, Inc.
Katonah, New York

A red-tailed hawk hurt her wing
and could not fly.

Beth found her at the edge
of the woods.

Beth took the hawk to the animal care
center and helped the veterinarian x-ray her.
The x-ray showed that the bone
in the hawk's wing was broken.

The veterinarian gave the hawk a shot
to help her sleep. They put a hood over
her head to keep her calm and taped
her down. A pin was put into the bone.
The wing was set and ready to heal.

Every day Beth went to the animal care center and fed the red-tailed hawk. The hawk ate mice.

Beth exercised the hawk's wing.

While the hawk lay on her back,
Beth opened the wing. She moved it
as if the hawk were flying.

After the wing healed,
Beth took the hawk out to fly.

The hawk could fly, but not very far.
Her wing was still weak.

She was not ready to be
on her own.

Beth took the hawk flying
again and again.

Weeks later, the hawk's wing
was strong. Now she was ready
to be on her own.

Beth released her.

And the red-tailed hawk
flew home.